D0719334

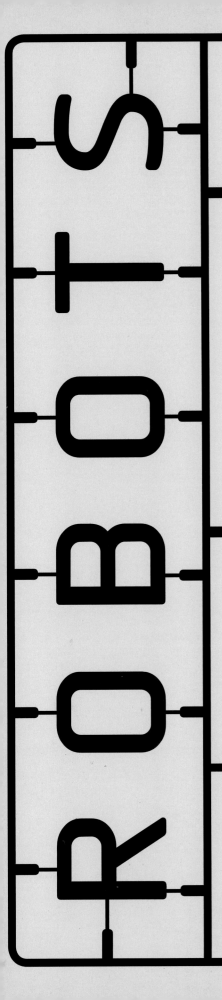

ROBOTS

ADVENTURES IN
STEAM

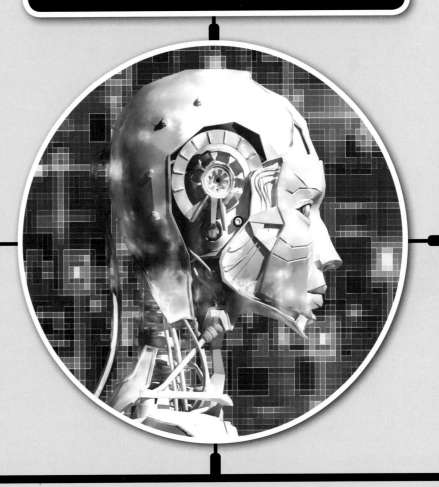

Izzi Howell

WAYLAND
www.waylandbooks.co.uk

First published in Great Britain in 2017 by Wayland

Series editor: Izzi Howell
Designer: Rocket Design (East Anglia) Ltd
Illustrations: Rocket Design (East Anglia) Ltd and Julian Baker
In-house editor: Julia Bird/Catherine Brereton

ISBN: 978 1 5263 0477 3
10 9 8 7 6 5 4 3 2 1

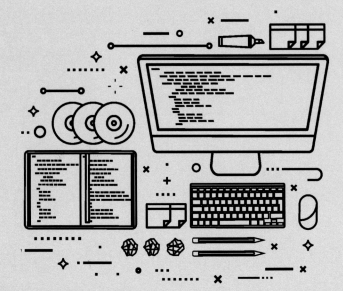

MIX
Paper from
responsible sources
FSC® C104740

Wayland
An imprint of
Hachette Children's Group
Part of Hodder & Stoughton
Carmelite House
50 Victoria Embankment
London EC4Y 0DZ

An Hachette UK Company
www.hachette.co.uk
www.hachettechildrens.co.uk

Printed in China

Picture acknowledgements:
Alamy: Xinhua 31c, REUTERS 32br and 33b, Paolo Patrizi 40; Dreamstime: Theowl84 11; iStock: VLADGRIN 19, JasonDoiy
29, CatLane 32bl, brittak 36t, Woodkern 45; Jean-Michel Mongeau, Ardian Jusufi and Pauline Jennings. Courtesy of
PolyPEDAL Lab UC Berkeley 6; Julian Baker 37; NASA: 27, NASA/JPL-Caltech/MSSS 30t; Shutterstock: NesaCera cover
and title page, OlegDoroshin 4, Designua 12, Alena Kirdina 13, Scanrail1 16, Christian Mueller 17, LANTERIA 18, Nataliya
Hora 20, Tatiana Shepeleva 21, Tim Jenner 22, Everett Historical 23b, Lerner Vadim 25, Miks Mihails Ignats, Alex
Tuzhikov, B Brown, anucha sirivisansuwan 28 l-r, catwalker 30b, chuckstock 31t, Quality Stock Arts 32t, CHEN WS 33tl,
iLoveCoffeeDesign 34, Tyler Olson 35, Aleks Melnik 36b, s_bukley 42t, Featureflash Photo Agency 42br, Sarunyu L 42bc,
Nicescene 42bl, Anton_Ivanov 43t, Phillip Maguire 43c, Wasan Ritthawon 43b, Ramona Kaulitzki 44; Wikimedia: Daderot
23t, Copyright Georgia Institute of Technology 2008/Rob Felt 24, Tactical Technology Office, Defense Advanced Research
Projects Agency, U.S. Department of Defense 31b, Sven Volkens 32c.

All design elements from Shutterstock.

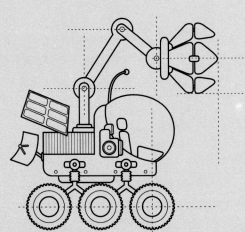

CONTENTS

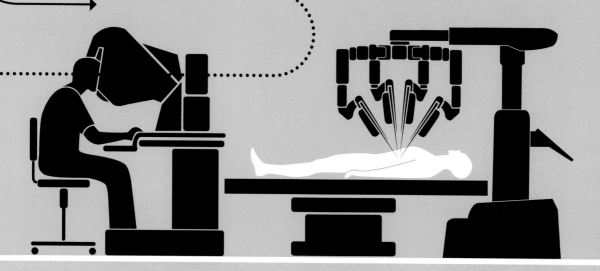

DESIGNING A ROBOT

A ROBOT IS A MACHINE THAT CAN BE PROGRAMMED TO ACT IN A CERTAIN WAY. ROBOTS USE SENSORS TO GATHER INFORMATION ABOUT THEIR ENVIRONMENT. THEY ARE PROGRAMMED TO USE THIS INFORMATION TO DECIDE HOW TO ACT.

Robots have many functions, helping humans with tasks as varied as working in factories, exploring the Antarctic and carrying out surgery. Whatever the final output of the robot, the planning process is the same.

STEP 1

CONCEPT
What is the purpose of the robot? What features does it need? What size does it need to be?

STEP 2

DESIGN
How will the robot fulfil the aims set out in the concept? What will it look like? How can we make the robot move in the right way? How can we programme it to behave correctly?

STEP 3

CREATION
How can the design be converted into a real robot? What parts do we need? How long will it take to put together?

The designers who created this robot wanted to make a robot that could draw a picture. This was their concept. In order to achieve this, they gave the robot parts that could hold and move a pen. Then, they programmed it to move in the correct way to create a drawing.

PROJECT

- Look at the photo of the robot that can draw. Adapt this robot so that it could paint a wall.

- Which parts of the robot need to change?

- Which parts can stay the same?

- How could you adapt it further so that it could paint *and* draw?

IT TAKES MANY DIFFERENT SKILLS TO DESIGN AND CREATE A ROBOT. SOME ROBOTS ARE MADE BY LARGE TEAMS OF PEOPLE, WHILE OTHERS ARE PUT TOGETHER BY ONE PERSON WORKING VERY HARD ON THEIR OWN!

1

Experts provide a brief for what they need the robot to be able to do.

2

Mechanical engineers design the body of the robot. They think about how it needs to move and how it can sense its environment.

3
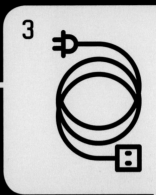

Electrical engineers design the electrical circuits that power the robot.

4

Software engineers programme the computer of the robot. Programming a robot means that it can react in the right way to information from its sensors.

5
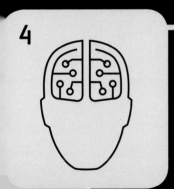

Mechanics put together the pieces that make up the robot and test that it is working properly.

TECHNOLOGY TALK

Computer programs make life easier for electrical and mechanical engineers, as they mean engineers can plan and test the structure and electrical circuits of a robot before it is built. 3D printers can also be used to print individual robot parts, whether they are large and difficult to construct or small and intricate.

MOVING PARTS

A ROBOT HAS MECHANICAL PARTS THAT FIT TOGETHER AND ALLOW IT TO MOVE, JUST LIKE THE SKELETON AND MUSCLES OF AN ANIMAL. THE WAY IN WHICH A ROBOT MOVES DEPENDS ON ITS FUNCTION AND THE PLACE WHERE IT WILL BE USED.

Every day, we move in thousands of subtle ways without giving much thought to how our bodies allow us to do so. Even a simple movement, such as picking up a pen, requires us to bend and stretch many connected bones and muscles. During the design process, mechanical engineers have to consider how a robot will need to interact with its environment. The robot will only be able to carry out complex movements if it has a mechanical structure that allows it to do so.

As well as moving to interact with objects, engineers have to plan how robots will get about. It is very complicated to create a robot that can walk on two feet. Rolling on wheels is much easier and quicker, but it has one big drawback – wheeled robots can't go up stairs.

The tiny, six-legged DASH robot can flip under a ledge and run along its underside, just like a cockroach. Its designers were inspired by the way that cockroaches can scramble over uneven ground, as they wanted to create a robot that could explore the rubble of collapsed buildings.

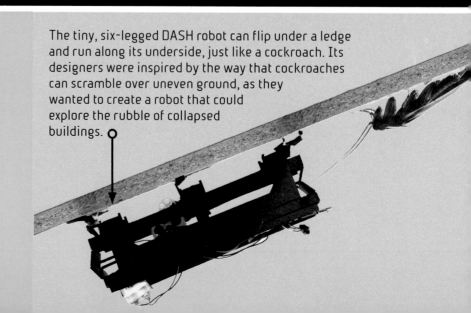

THINKING OUTSIDE THE BOX!

Scientists have designed other robots that mimic the way that animals move. For example, the underwater exploration robot Crabster 200 crawls along the ocean floor like a crab. It can adjust the position of each of its six legs individually to keep its balance in strong ocean currents.

"MATHS TALK

Engineers use triangles to work out the angle at which robot arms need to bend. If you mark a point at the top of a robot arm, the middle of the arm joint and at the point the robot needs to reach, it forms a triangle.

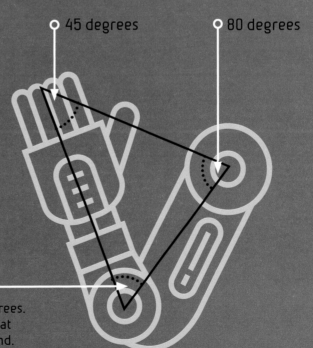

45 degrees

80 degrees

All the angles in a triangle add up to 180 degrees. Use this information to work out the angle that the elbow joint of this robot arm needs to bend."

 # CIRCUITS

IF MECHANICAL PARTS ARE THE SKELETON AND MUSCLES OF A ROBOT, ELECTRICITY IS ITS BLOOD. ELECTRICITY GIVES ROBOTS THE POWER TO MOVE AND CARRY OUT ACTIONS.

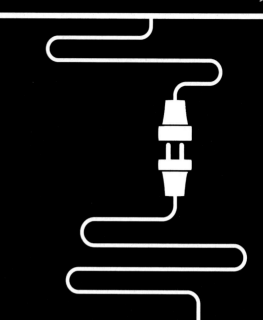

Most robots are fitted with electrical cables that carry electricity around the machine and power its components. These cables are arranged in circuits. If a circuit is not complete, electricity will not flow around the robot and it will stop working.

SCIENCE TALK

Circuits can be arranged in series or in parallel. In a series circuit, all components are on the same loop. This means that if one component breaks, the whole circuit stops working. In a parallel circuit, each component is on a separate loop. The circuit will keep working, even if one component breaks.

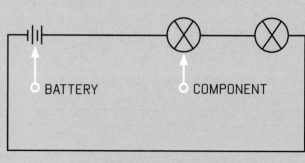

BATTERY   COMPONENT

SERIES CIRCUIT

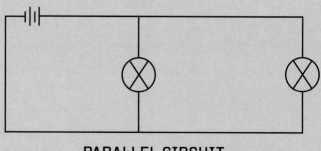

PARALLEL CIRCUIT

Robots need to be connected to a power source that will send electricity around their circuits. Plugging a robot into an electrical socket is an easy way of accessing a lot of electricity, but it does limit the movement of the robot, as it can't move too far away from the socket. Battery-powered robots can travel freely, but their batteries will eventually need to be recharged or replaced.

Small robots can be powered by household batteries.

THINKING OUTSIDE THE BOX!

Robots in space can't connect to mains electricity or have their batteries replaced, so they often run on solar power instead. The solar panels on the robot convert light from the Sun into a constant supply of electricity, as long as the robot isn't covered or in darkness. Some robots can also get energy from food. Scientists have created prototypes for a grass-eating lawnmower robot and a slug-eating robot, which would be very popular with gardeners!

SENSORS

MOST ROBOTS HAVE ELECTRICAL SENSORS, WHICH THEY USE TO GATHER INFORMATION ABOUT THE WORLD AROUND THEM, JUST AS HUMANS DO THROUGH OUR SENSES. SOME ROBOTS CAN EVEN SENSE THINGS THAT HUMANS CANNOT, SUCH AS X-RAYS AND MAGNETISM!

A sensor is a device that gathers information. Not all sensors are electrical – for example, an ear is a biological sensor that humans and animals use to sense sounds, or hear. Instead of ears, robots use microphones to sense sounds around them.

TECHNOLOGY TALK

To sense sounds, a robot records a noise with its microphone and converts it into signals that show the pitch and strength of the sound. The robot's computer then looks through a database of sound patterns to recognise the words or type of noise. This process is the same as that used by the voice recognition software on your home computer or smartphone.

This diagram shows the sound waves produced by a person speaking. This is the type of pattern that computers analyse to identify what someone is saying. This pattern shows someone saying 'I love you'. Can you work out where each word appears in the pattern?

Proprioception, or the sense of your own movement and position, is a little-known yet highly important sense for humans and robots alike. Robots can build up an idea of how they are moving by measuring their own speed and rotation, and using pressure sensors to monitor things that they are touching.

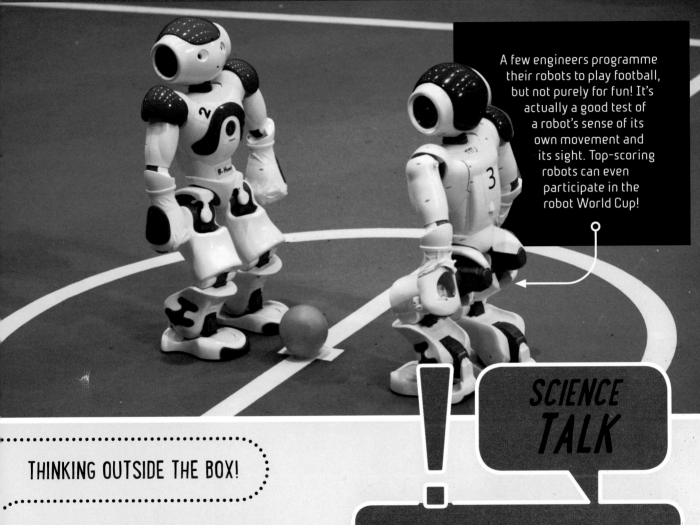

A few engineers programme their robots to play football, but not purely for fun! It's actually a good test of a robot's sense of its own movement and its sight. Top-scoring robots can even participate in the robot World Cup!

SCIENCE TALK

THINKING OUTSIDE THE BOX!

Any sensor that can be built can be added to a robot, giving robots an almost unlimited possible number of senses! Robots can be given magnetometers to spot magnetic materials, thermal cameras to sense temperature and mass spectrometers to identify rocks. They can even identify types of wave from the electromagnetic spectrum that humans can't see, such as radio waves and X-rays.

Our sense of smell is actually just chemistry, as sensors in the nose recognise the tiny chemical molecules given off by objects. Robots with similar electrical sensors can recognise smells in the same way. The Mexican scientist Blanca Lorena Villareal has gone a step further, and is developing a robot that is programmed to follow certain smells, such as blood and sweat during search and rescue missions.

SIGHT AND NAVIGATION

SOME ROBOTS NEED TO BE ABLE TO NAVIGATE THEIR PHYSICAL ENVIRONMENT, SO THAT HUMANS DON'T HAVE TO MANUALLY DIRECT THEM. GIVING ROBOTS THE SENSE OF SIGHT ISN'T THE ONLY WAY OF ACHIEVING THIS. SOUND CAN ALSO BE A USEFUL NAVIGATIONAL TOOL.

One way to give robots a sense of what is around them is to use sonar. In sonar, a sender makes a noise and sends out a sound wave. The sound wave bounces off nearby objects and is reflected back to the sender. The sender's sensor (such as an ear) interprets the reflected sound wave and builds up a picture of its physical environment. Self-driving cars, which mainly use GPS to navigate the roads, also have sonar to warn them of unexpected obstacles!

THINKING OUTSIDE THE BOX!

Scientists often find ideas for new projects in nature. The inspiration for sonar came from animals that naturally use sonar, or echolocation, for navigation and to find food. Bats use echolocation to search for insects to eat while they are hunting at night. Echolocation also helps dolphins and porpoises to find fish underwater where vision is limited.

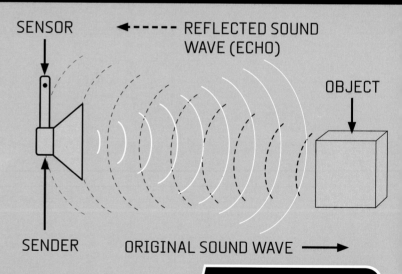

SENSOR

◀----- REFLECTED SOUND WAVE (ECHO)

OBJECT

SENDER

ORIGINAL SOUND WAVE ➝

PROJECT

- Try using echolocation to navigate around a room. Blindfold yourself and communicate with a partner, who is hiding, by using sound. When you say a word, your partner must echo it back. See how long it takes for you to find your partner.

- How can you tell when your partner is far away?

- What does it sound like when your partner is close?

- Which objects in the room confuse your sense of where your partner is?

Sonar and GPS let robots know that there are objects around them, but they can't help robots identify what these objects are. Some robots can be programmed to use visual information from a camera to recognise objects. While human brains can automatically identify a familiar object on sight, robots need to be taught what shapes to look out for, as well as the names that we give these objects.

ENGINEERING TALK

If a robot sees a 12-cm-tall cylinder, it can consult its database to deduce that the object is a drinks can. However, if the can is crushed or at a different angle, the robot will struggle to recognise it, while a human would still be able to.

If a person sees a table from any angle, they automatically recognise it as a table. However, a robot will need to be taught to recognise the combination of shapes as a table. Engineers do this by programming robots with a database of information, which describes many possible shapes and their meaning.

CODE

COMPLEX COMPUTER PROGRAMMING IS WHAT SETS ROBOTS APART FROM SIMPLE MACHINES, SUCH AS HAIR DRYERS. COMPUTERS ARE THE 'BRAINS' OF ROBOTS, TELLING THEM WHAT TO DO AND HOW TO DO IT.

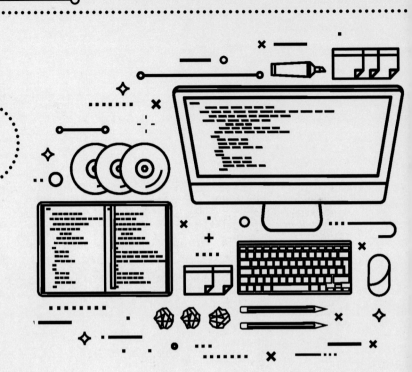

Software engineers write instructions for computers using code, a special type of language. Anything that is connected to a computer, from computer games and phone apps to robots, runs on code.

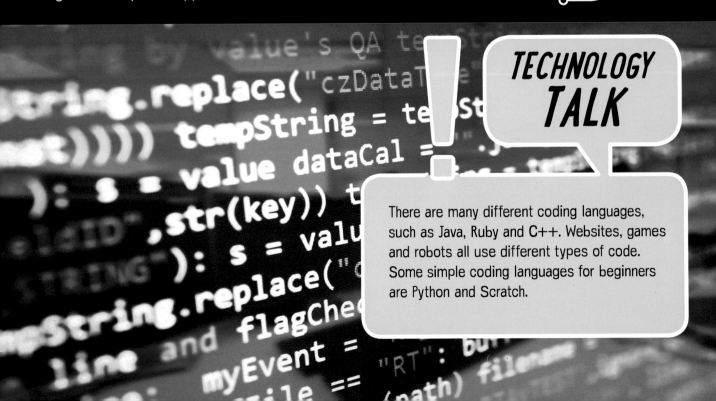

TECHNOLOGY TALK

There are many different coding languages, such as Java, Ruby and C++. Websites, games and robots all use different types of code. Some simple coding languages for beginners are Python and Scratch.

CARRY OUT TASKS.

When a coder writes instructions for a task for a robot, the instructions have to be broken down into small steps. For example, rather than saying 'make toast', you would need to explain step by step exactly how to make toast. Computers won't do anything unless you instruct them to, so it's important to include everything that you want them to do.

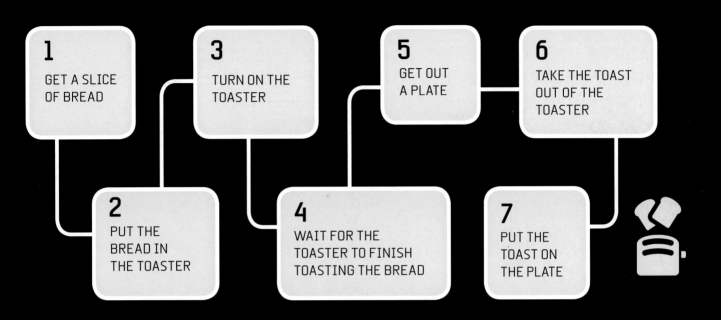

1 GET A SLICE OF BREAD

2 PUT THE BREAD IN THE TOASTER

3 TURN ON THE TOASTER

4 WAIT FOR THE TOASTER TO FINISH TOASTING THE BREAD

5 GET OUT A PLATE

6 TAKE THE TOAST OUT OF THE TOASTER

7 PUT THE TOAST ON THE PLATE

"MATHS TALK

Computers need to be told the order in which to carry out their instructions, or the task will go wrong! This is the same in maths, when you work out long equations with multiple operations. For example, the answer to 5+2x4 could be 28 or 13, depending on whether you add or multiply first. The rules of operations state that you should do multiplication or division first and then addition or subtraction. What is the correct answer to 5+2x4?

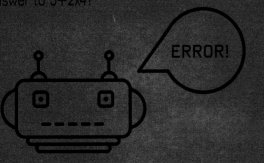

ERROR!

PROJECT

- Write a code for an activity that you do every day, such as brushing your teeth or making your bed. Make sure that you break down every step.

- How many steps does it take?

- How easy would it be for a robot to follow your instructions?

PROGRAMMING ROBOTS

THE COMPUTER INSIDE A ROBOT IS PROGRAMMED TO MAKE DECISIONS USING INFORMATION GATHERED FROM ITS SENSORS. ROBOTS CAN ONLY CHOOSE TO DO THINGS THAT THEY HAVE BEEN PROGRAMMED TO DO, RATHER THAN RESPONDING INSTINCTIVELY TO A SITUATION.

The way in which robots are programmed to make decisions is just like a flow chart. The stages of the flow chart show different decisions that a robot could make. For example, this flow chart shows how a robot could be programmed to cross the road.

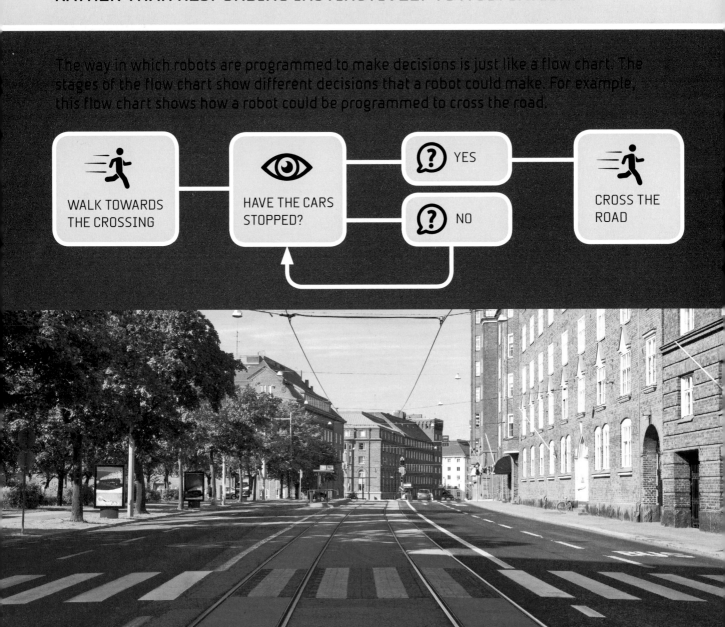

WALK TOWARDS THE CROSSING

HAVE THE CARS STOPPED?

? YES

? NO

CROSS THE ROAD

Computer programmers describe decision-making moments using IFTTT statements (if this, then that). For example, if there are no cars, then cross the road. Most robots are programmed with hundreds of IFTTT statements that help them to react appropriately to every possible situation. Being programmed with multiple IFTTT statements would help the road-crossing robot to know what to do in less usual situations, such as someone standing in your way on the crossing.

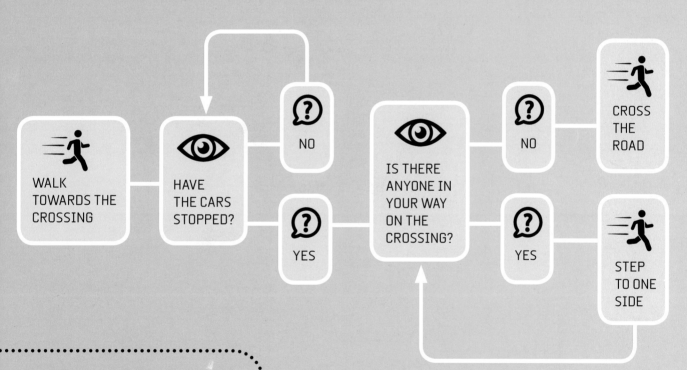

WALK TOWARDS THE CROSSING → HAVE THE CARS STOPPED? → NO / YES

IS THERE ANYONE IN YOUR WAY ON THE CROSSING? → NO → CROSS THE ROAD / YES → STEP TO ONE SIDE

THINKING OUTSIDE THE BOX!

We can't always anticipate all potential problems, so some robots need to be programmed to respond independently to things going wrong. Space rovers and robots in hostile environments far from humans are programmed to try random actions if they break or get stuck, as eventually something should work!

ARTIFICIAL INTELLIGENCE

ARTIFICIAL INTELLIGENCE IS ONE OF THE MOST IMPORTANT AND MOST CONTROVERSIAL AREAS OF ROBOTICS RESEARCH. MANY PEOPLE WONDER IF WE CAN OR SHOULD CREATE ROBOTS THAT CAN THINK FOR THEMSELVES.

It is hard to compare human and robot intelligence, because they are both intelligent in different ways. Humans are intelligent because they can learn, reason, use language and come up with new ideas. Robots can be programmed to be intelligent in some of these ways, such as learning. They learn by identifying and recording the results of a specific action. They know that if they repeat the action, it will have the same result. However, robots also have their own forms of intelligence, such as the ability to calculate complicated mathematical equations that most humans would never be able to solve.

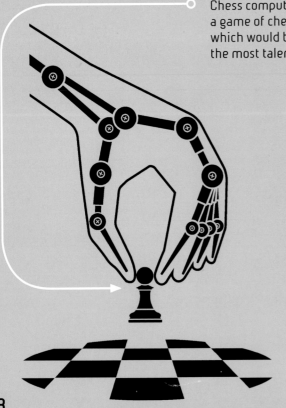

Chess computers are programmed to use reason to choose the best move in a game of chess. They can consider the consequences of all possible moves, which would be very hard for a human to do. Chess computers can beat even the most talented human chess players.

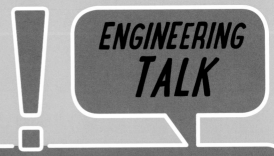

ENGINEERING TALK

The human brain is made up of an incredibly sophisticated network of electrical signals. Engineers believe that if they can create a complete map of the human brain and fully understand how it works, they might be able to create an artificial brain with a similar level of intelligence one day.

The Turing Test is a way of testing the intelligence of a robot. In the test, a human puts questions to another human and a robot via a computer screen, and tries to guess which is which. If the question-asker can't identify the human, the robot has passed the test. The problem with the Turing Test is that it only tests whether robots can successfully imitate human ways of thinking, not whether they can be programmed to truly think and feel for themselves.

TECHNOLOGY TALK

Most of the robots entered into the Turing Test are chatbots – robots that are programmed to respond to standard questions by recognising keywords and taking answers from a database. They are often used as automated customer service assistants to help people with simple problems online. Advanced chatbots learn more language from each conversation that they have with humans.

PROJECT

- Try chatting to a chatbot, such as the one found at http://alice.pandorabots.com/.

- Which type of question can the chatbot answer easily?

- Can you find a question that confuses the chatbot? Why is it confusing?

- What would be the difference between the chatbot's responses and a human's responses to the same questions?

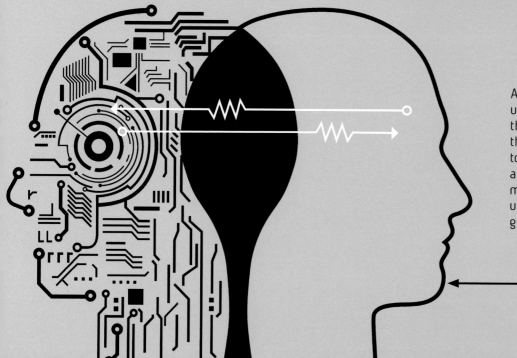

Although robots can't yet understand language in the same way as humans, they can be programmed to reply to speech in a relevant way. This makes it seem as if they understand what's going on!

ROBOT ETHICS

SCIENCE AND TECHNOLOGY OFTEN RAISE ETHICAL QUESTIONS, AS TRYING TO .... CONTROL NATURE MAY DO MORE HARM THAN GOOD. THERE ARE MANY ETHICAL DEBATES RELATED TO ROBOTICS, AS SOME PEOPLE WORRY ABOUT THE RESULTS OF CREATING ARTIFICIAL INTELLIGENCE.

Robots have already replaced thousands of human jobs in factories, such as in this car factory. If robots take over other types of job as well, it could have a devastating effect on employment around the world.

The main questions around robotics relate to the difference between humans and robots with advanced artificial intelligence. If we create robots that are as clever as humans, should the robots have the same rights as humans? Can we throw intelligent robots away if they are broken? Some people even fear that robots may one day become more intelligent than humans, and threaten to take over human civilisation! However, as scientists are yet to develop the technology that people are worrying about, we have no real answers to these questions for now.

MATHS TALK

Many industries are switching from human workers to robots in their factories. Although it costs more money to buy robots at the start, it ends up being much cheaper than employing a human, as people need to be paid a regular salary. If an industrial robot costs £50,000 to buy and a factory worker's salary is £1,200 a month, how many months will it take before investment in the robot is less than the total amount of money paid to a human worker?

Some people think that the key to resolving these ethical dilemmas lies in the way that we programme robots. As humans are in charge of programming all robots, even super-intelligent ones, we can choose not to create robots that might put humans in danger. However, this is a hard idea for some scientists to grasp, as the thrill of making a breakthrough overshadows the consequences of what they have created.

THINKING OUTSIDE THE BOX!

Isaac Asimov was a scientist and author who wrote many stories about robots. In one of his stories, he introduced the idea of the Three Laws of Robotics – rules programmed into a robot's software that are designed to protect humans and ensure good robot behaviour. Some people think that similar rules could help us to control super-intelligent robots in the future.

Many science fiction stories revolve around armies of robots rising up against humans, but this is very unlikely to happen in real life.

ASIMOV'S THREE LAWS OF ROBOTICS

FIRST LAW

A robot may not injure a human being or, through inaction, allow a human being to come to harm.

SECOND LAW

A robot must obey orders given to it by human beings, except where such orders would conflict with the First Law.

THIRD LAW

A robot must protect its own existence, as long as such protection does not conflict with the First or Second Laws.

THE FIRST ROBOTS

IN THE 18TH AND 19TH CENTURIES, THE ARRIVAL OF THE INDUSTRIAL REVOLUTION AND ELECTRICITY PAVED THE WAY FOR ROBOTICS. HOWEVER, IT WASN'T UNTIL THE 20TH CENTURY, AND THE RISE OF COMPUTERS AND COMPUTER PROGRAMMING, THAT THE FIRST ROBOTS BEGAN TO EMERGE.

For most of history, objects were made by hand, which was a time-consuming and expensive process. During the Industrial Revolution, people developed new machines that could manufacture objects for them, saving them time and money. Over time, we became able to create more advanced machines, such as robots, that could do lots of work with very little human input.

THINKING OUTSIDE THE BOX!

Weaving was one of the first industries to incorporate machines. Mechanical looms worked much faster than human weavers. In 1804, Joseph Jacquard developed the Jacquard loom – a machine that used sequences of punched cards to control the pattern of the woven fabric. This invention inspired Charles Babbage, an early computer programmer. Babbage planned to use a similar system of punched cards to control his Analytical Engine, a type of early mechanical computer.

This is a modern model of one of Babbage's designs. The number wheels moved around, allowing the machine to carry out complicated mathematical equations.

As scientists learned how to handle electricity in the late 19th century, more and more machines were adapted to run off this new power source, including the very simple first robots. One of the first electrical robots, Elektro, appeared at the World Fair in New York in 1939. Elektro could walk and move its arms and legs, thanks to motors. An internal record player allowed him to respond to certain simple voice commands.

Elektro later appeared with a robot dog, Sparko, that could sit, bark and beg.

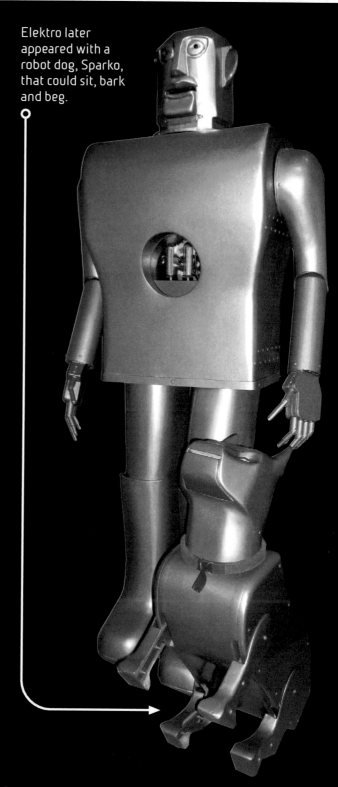

TECHNOLOGY TALK

The development of modern computers and computer programming in the 1940s and 50s allowed robotics to flourish. Engineers learned how to harness the power of a computer to control robots for different purposes. In 1954, the first industrial robot, Unimate, was introduced. Unimate was a programmable robot arm that could remove and stack hot metal parts in a factory.

The first computers were much larger than the computers we use today! This photo shows the ENAIC computer, one of the first general-purpose computers, which was created in 1946.

ROBOTS IN DANGER

MANY JOBS CARRIED OUT BY ROBOTS ARE CONSIDERED TOO BORING AND REPETITIVE FOR HUMANS. HOWEVER, ROBOTS ARE ALSO ON THE FRONTLINE IN SOME OF THE MOST DANGEROUS PLACES ON EARTH, WHERE HUMANS WOULD STRUGGLE TO SURVIVE.

Bomb-disposal robots have mechanical arms to pick up and inspect suspicious packages.

Scientists often use robots to gather data in areas that humans can't reach, such as inside volcanoes or deep underwater trenches. The data collected by these robots is crucial for scientists and, one day, might help them find evidence to explain things that we don't understand well, such as exactly how volcanoes erupt.

This looks like a toy, but it's actually a NASA SnoMote robot. This robot takes measurements in remote polar regions, which scientists study to try to understand why the ice is melting so fast in these areas.

SCIENCE TALK

Using robots to gather data for experiments can help to make it a fair test. When people carry out experiments, it's possible that they might accidentally do something differently each time, which would affect the end result. As robots can't change their behaviour unless they are programmed to do so, the conditions of a robot-led experiment will always be the same. This keeps results accurate.

Robots can also be used to resolve very dangerous situations, where human lives would be at risk. They are routinely used to dispose of bombs and find landmines, and have been used to explore areas affected by nuclear power plant disasters. Tiny robots can also squeeze into small gaps in the rubble of collapsed buildings to look for survivors.

This bomb-disposal robot in Jerusalem is investigating an abandoned bag, in case it contains explosive material.

THINKING OUTSIDE THE BOX!

When designing a robot, it can help to think about who or what typically uses the environment where the robot will be operated. For example, a robot designed to clear up nuclear waste in a nuclear power plant will need to move through an environment designed for humans: walking up stairs, opening doors with handles and using tools designed for humans. As a result, this robot probably needs to be humanoid, with jointed legs to walk up stairs and jointed fingers to hold door handles and tools.

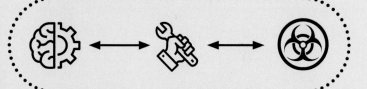

PROJECT

- Design a robot that can explore the peaks of extremely high mountains.

- Which animals live high on mountains? How can you use their movement and body shape as inspiration?

- What kind of sensors would work best in mountainous conditions?

ROBOTS IN SPACE

HUMANS USE ROBOTS TO EXPLORE AREAS OF OUTER SPACE THAT THEY ARE NOT YET ABLE TO VISIT. ROBOTIC ROVERS HAVE VISITED THE SURFACE OF THE MOON, MARS AND VENUS, AS WELL AS SEVERAL ASTEROIDS AND COMETS.

Space rovers are robotic vehicles that explore, take measurements and snap photos. They can analyse the chemical composition of rock samples, so that scientists on Earth know what the surface is made of without having to travel into space! Many rovers are powered by radioactive materials, as it can be risky to depend on solar power. The Philae lander went into hibernation mode after landing in a shady area on a comet, where it couldn't get enough sunlight to power itself.

" MATHS TALK

Scientists communicate with rovers in space via radio waves. However, as most bodies in space are very far away from Earth, it takes a long time for radio waves to arrive, so scientists can't control rovers in real time. Most rover activity is automated or programmed in advance. We can use a distance/speed/time triangle to work out how long communication will take.

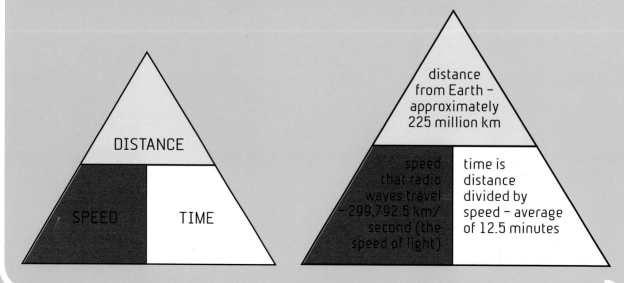

As scientists do not always have a complete understanding of the type of environment that a rover will be exploring, they need to prepare the robot to move over different types of surface. Most rovers have large wheels that work well on rugged, rocky ground. Engineers are also experimenting with other types of movement, such as a jumping robot that could leap out of deep sand.

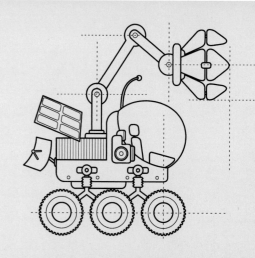

Robonaut is a humanoid robot that works on the International Space Station. He has fully functioning fingers that allow him to do many of the same tasks as the astronauts.

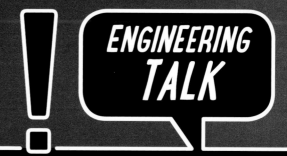

THINKING OUTSIDE THE BOX!

It would be risky not to test rovers, but it is expensive and time-consuming to test them in space. Instead, engineers test robots (and train astronauts) in places called analogue sites, where the conditions are very similar to space. Analogue sites can be icy or boiling hot to match different space temperatures, with sandy, rocky or steep surfaces to mimic a planet's surface.

! ENGINEERING TALK

Rovers are designed to be able to fix themselves, as there are no humans around to repair them if they break down in space! For example, if the drill head on the Mars Curiosity rover gets stuck in a rock, the drill arm spits it out. The drill arm then picks up a replacement drill head from a storage box, pops it into place and keeps on drilling!

DRONES AND CARS

THE IDEA OF LETTING ROBOTIC VEHICLES NAVIGATE OUR ROADS AND AIRWAYS IS BECOMING MORE AND MORE ACCEPTABLE. DRONES AND SELF-DRIVING CARS CAN HUGELY BENEFIT HUMANS, BUT THERE IS ALWAYS A RISK INVOLVED.

A drone is an aircraft without a pilot on board. Most drones are controlled remotely by programming in a GPS location and letting the drone work out its own way to get there. At first, drones were mainly used by the military to carry out surveillance, transport weapons and drop bombs. As drones have become cheaper and more available, they have been used in other ways, such as to deliver items, carry out research or just for fun.

Can you identify the landscapes shown in these aerial photos taken by drones?

" ART TALK

Videos mounted on drones have captured amazing aerial images that show us the world from an often unseen angle. Many landscapes look quite abstract when seen from above, as we focus on the shapes and patterns in the landscape. These images could be an interesting starting point for a piece of abstract art. "

In theory, self-driving cars are advanced enough to be able to navigate the streets on their own, but for safety reasons, there are no driverless cars on the streets yet. For now, engineers are testing self-driving cars with humans behind the wheel who can take over just in case! However, self-driving cars have been involved in several crashes and one fatal accident in which the human back-up driver died. So, scientists still have some way to go.

Google is investing lots of money in self-driving cars, and is aiming to make them available to the public by 2020.

ENGINEERING TALK

Self-driving cars have various sensors that enable them to find their way around the roads. They use cameras to recognise signs, radar to work out the space between them and nearby vehicles, and lasers to gather data on the car's surroundings. These sensors send data to the onboard computer, which is programmed to decide how to drive the car and will instruct it to slow down or speed up if necessary.

HALL OF FAME: REAL ROBOTS

CURIOSITY ROVER

The world's most famous robotic rover, NASA's Curiosity, is currently exploring Mars. It is looking for evidence of water and checking if Mars might have the right conditions for life to have existed there in the past or for humans to survive there in the future. NASA streams footage from Curiosity's adventures on the Internet, which many people on Earth have enjoyed watching. On the first anniversary of Curiosity's stay on Mars, it played the song 'Happy Birthday', which was the first time a song was played on another planet.

ASIMO

ASIMO is one of the most advanced humanoid robots. It is used in public demonstrations around the world as an example of what can be achieved in robotics. ASIMO has two legs and can walk and run, which is a huge achievement in robotics. It can also recognise gestures, sounds and faces, and use this information to interact meaningfully with humans.

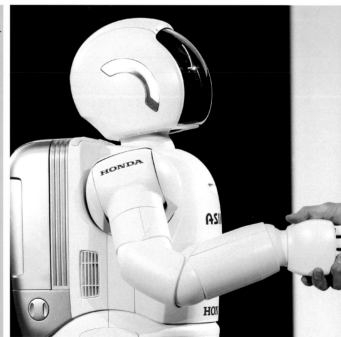

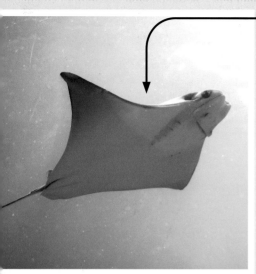

ROBOTIC STINGRAY

This real stingray was the inspiration for a cyborg (a robot with biological parts). The robotic stingray has over 200,000 genetically engineered rat heart-muscle cells on its underside. When the heart cells contract (as heart cells do, in order to pump blood around the body), the movement pushes the stingray forwards in the water! The heart cells are also genetically engineered so that they only contract in certain light. Scientists can control where the robot moves by shining light in different places. They hope that they will learn more about how the heart pumps blood from experiments with the robot.

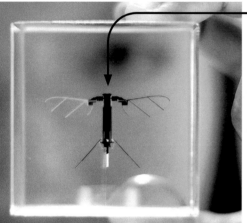

ROBOBEE

These mini robots, weighing less than one-tenth of a gram and measuring half the length of a paper clip, could revolutionise search and rescue missions, surveillance and even help to pollinate fields of crops. Robobees are able to act as a group and coordinate their behaviour, just like a swarm of real bees. Their tiny wings are made of a ceramic material that expands and contracts when electricity passes through it, creating a flapping motion and keeping the robot in the air.

LS3

This powerful robot is designed to carry equipment for soldiers (LS3 stands for Legged Squad Support System). Similar to a horse, the LS3 can follow a leader through all terrain, avoid obstacles and carry over 180 kg of weight. Having a helper to carry equipment keeps soldiers from getting tired or hurting themselves before the fighting has even begun!

WHILE THE LATEST DEVELOPMENTS IN ROBOTICS DAZZLE US ON TV AND IN NEWSPAPER REPORTS, EQUALLY IMPRESSIVE ROBOTS CAN ALSO BE FOUND IN OUR HOMES. ROBOTIC TOYS, HOUSEHOLD APPLIANCES AND COMPANIONS BRING CONVENIENCE AND ENJOYMENT TO OUR DAY-TO-DAY LIVES.

ROOMBA

The Roomba is an autonomous robot vacuum cleaner. It's actually quite unusual to have a fully autonomous robot – most robots are semi-autonomous for safety reasons. However, the Roomba is so small that it isn't considered a risk to let it do its own thing! It uses sensors to detect especially dirty areas and know when to change direction, and can even sense deep drops to stop it falling down stairs.

PARO THE SEAL

In some hospitals and nursing homes, Paro robot seals are given to patients to soothe them and keep them company. Paro can seek out eye contact and respond to stroking and sounds, including its own name. It is covered in soft white fur that people love to touch!

FURBY

These adorable, fluffy toys are actually tiny robots! Although Furbies start out speaking only in Furbish, a unique Furby language, their internal computer is programmed to learn English through interaction with humans. A simple motor system allows the Furby to raise its eyelids and ears and open its mouth.

LEGO™ MINDSTORMS

This range of Lego™ kits contains the software and hardware needed to build your own robot, such as a mini computer, sensors, motors and circuits. Many people consider that the best way to learn about robots is by building them yourself with kits, such as Lego™ Mindstorms.

AIBO

This robotic dog, designed to behave just like a real pet, was released in 1999. AIBOs could run and jump, react to their surroundings and show emotions, such as joy, making them excellent stand-ins for live dogs, despite their US $2000 price tag. Unfortunately, the company that made AIBOs stopped production in 2006 and won't repair old ones, giving these potentially immortal pets a much shorter lifespan.

JIBO

The social robot Jibo is not yet on the market, but is creating a lot of buzz! Designed by Cynthia Breazeal, a pioneer in the field of robot-human social interaction, Jibo is programmed to have meaningful social interactions with people and become a real part of the family. As well as keeping track of appointments, it can tell stories, take photos and recognise faces and voices.

ROBOTS AND MEDICINE

USING ROBOTS IN MEDICINE CAN HELP TO MAKE SURGERY AND MEDICAL PROCEDURES SAFER, CHEAPER AND MORE EFFICIENT. HOWEVER, DOCTORS HAVE TO TAKE SERIOUS CARE, AS A ROBOT BREAKING DOWN COULD THREATEN SOMEONE'S LIFE.

The da Vinci surgical robot is one of the most successful medical robots, with over 3,000 models used in hospitals around the world. It is used for keyhole surgery – a type of surgery in which tools are pushed through a very small hole in the skin to reach areas deep inside the body. The da Vinci robot is incredibly precise and will never shake or get distracted, unlike a human surgeon.

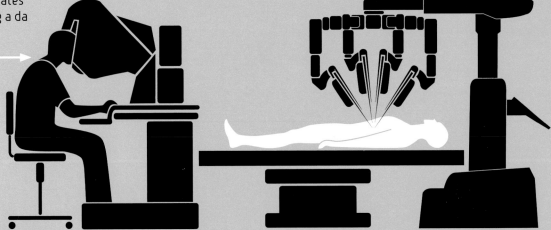

A surgeon operates on a patient using a da Vinci robot.

PROJECT

■ The da Vinci robot is so accurate that it can stitch a grape back together after it has been cut open. Ask an adult to help you cut a grape open and then try stitching it back together with a needle and thread.

■ How easy is it?

■ What features could a robot have that would make it better at this type of activity than a human?

THINKING OUTSIDE THE BOX!

Safety is a big concern with medical robots. Most robots can't make autonomous decisions and can only respond in the way that they have been programmed to, so who would be held responsible if something went wrong? To avoid this ethical conundrum, surgeons control surgical robots at all times. Robots that transport medicine around hospitals are programmed with codes and fingerprint sensors so that the medicine will only be released to the correct recipient.

TECHNOLOGY TALK

Surgeons control surgical robots using a telemanipulator or a computer. A telemanipulator is a device that transmits movements made by the surgeon to the robot electronically or mechanically. Surgeons can also control robots directly through a computer. This is particularly useful, as it means that the surgeon is able to be thousands of kilometres away from the robot!

Robots are useful when training doctors.
Instead of using real patients, trainee doctors can practise on patient simulator robots, which can breathe, bleed and sweat just like a human! They can also mimic the symptoms of a heart attack or a fit. Practising on robots reduces the risk to real patients, as there are no consequences if the trainee doctor makes a mistake.

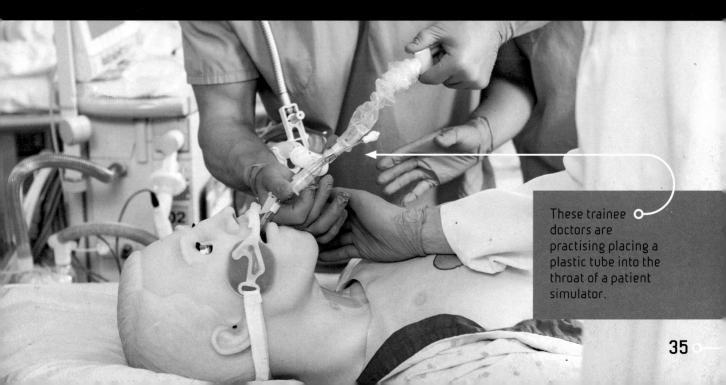

These trainee doctors are practising placing a plastic tube into the throat of a patient simulator.

BIONICS

BIONICS ARE ROBOTIC REPLACEMENTS FOR BIOLOGICAL BODY PARTS. ADVANCES IN BIONICS ARE ON TRACK TO REVOLUTIONISE MEDICINE. FOR EXAMPLE, IF WE COULD CREATE ROBOTIC ORGANS, WE WOULD NOT NEED TO DEPEND ON HUMAN DONORS.

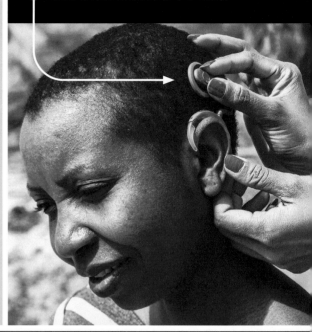

The microphone of the cochlear implant is fitted on the outside of the head.

The cochlear implant is one of the most commonly used bionics. Instead of standard hearing aids, which just make sounds louder, cochlear implants allow people with hearing problems to hear. A microphone in the implant picks up sounds and converts them into electrical impulses. The implant then sends the impulses to the brain, where they are interpreted as sounds.

SCIENCE TALK

Sounds are waves of vibrations that travel through the air and into our ears. The snail-shaped cochlea inside the ear carries out the same function as a cochlear implant — converting vibrations into signals, which are sent to the brain and understood as sound.

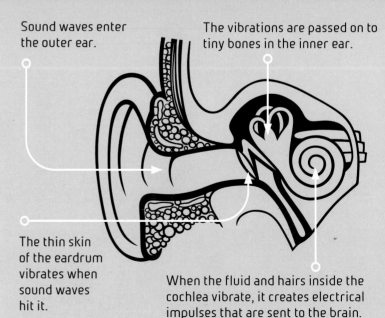

Sound waves enter the outer ear.

The vibrations are passed on to tiny bones in the inner ear.

The thin skin of the eardrum vibrates when sound waves hit it.

When the fluid and hairs inside the cochlea vibrate, it creates electrical impulses that are sent to the brain.

Bionic eyes work using an implant in the retina (the inner layer of the surface of the eye). They can help people who have lost vision due to illness. The implant receives visual information from a miniature camera, worn as part of a pair of glasses, which it then passes on to the brain. The bionic eye is still being developed and can't see detailed images just yet, but it can recognise outlines – a great step forward!

BEFORE

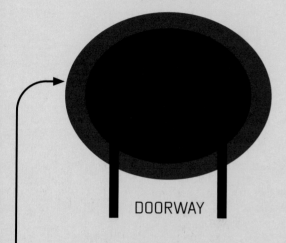

DOORWAY

Someone with vision loss due to illness wouldn't be able to see the line of a doorway. Everything would appear black.

AFTER

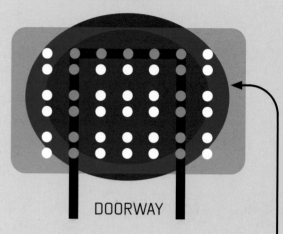

DOORWAY

After being fitted with a bionic eye, someone with vision loss would be able to make out the shape of a doorway (blue dots) against a wall (white dots).

SCIENCE TALK

The bionic artificial heart is currently being used as a temporary measure while people wait for a heart transplant. The engineering behind it is very simple, as the heart is essentially a pump! When it squeezes in, blood is pushed out around the body.

PROJECT

- Design a bionic lung.
- What are the functions of the lung?
- How would the lung work mechanically?
- What materials would you make the lung from?

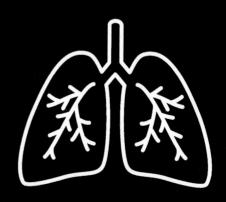

ROBOTIC ARMS

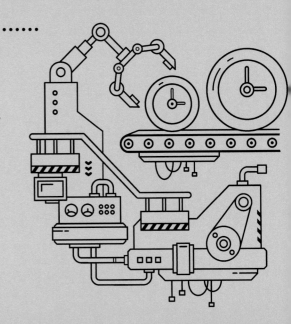

ROBOTS IN FACTORIES AND ASSEMBLY LINES OFTEN NEED TO BE ABLE TO PICK UP OBJECTS. ENGINEERS BUILD ROBOTS WITH SIMPLIFIED VERSIONS OF HUMAN HANDS, WHICH ARE CONTROLLED BY COMPUTERS TO MAKE THE ROBOT GRASP AND GRIP.

The human hand is pretty unbeatable as a tool, so it's easy to understand why engineers have copied its design. The twenty-seven bones in the hand give us a wide range of movements. The sensors on the tip of our fingers send signals to the brain that give us important information about the objects that we touch.

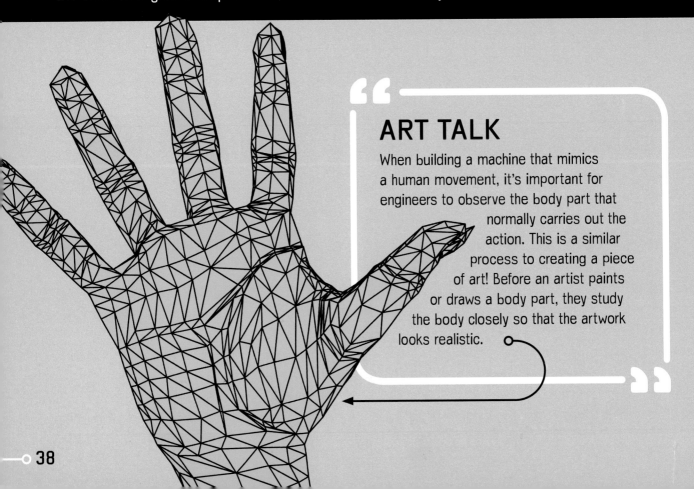

ART TALK

When building a machine that mimics a human movement, it's important for engineers to observe the body part that normally carries out the action. This is a similar process to creating a piece of art! Before an artist paints or draws a body part, they study the body closely so that the artwork looks realistic.

THINKING OUTSIDE THE BOX!

It would be unnecessary and expensive to give a complex robotic hand to a robot that has a simple task, such as picking up bottles. Instead, engineers give robots basic versions of human hands, with two or three 'fingers' to pinch and hold, or special attachments, such as hooks, suction cups or magnets!

One step beyond the robotic hand is the robotic prosthetic arm, which can replace a limb lost through disease or injury. Instead of being controlled by a computer, robotic prosthetic arms are directly controlled by the human brain. Thoughts from the brain are captured and turned into movement (see Techno Talk). The arm can also feel and touch, which helps the user to interact with their surroundings.

TECHNO TALK

Wires connect a robotic prosthetic arm with the motor cortex of the brain, which controls muscle movement. Thoughts from the brain, which are tiny electric charges, travel down the wires and make the arm move. When the fingers touch something, the arm sends electrical signals to the sensory cortex in the brain, which interprets the signals as the feeling of touch.

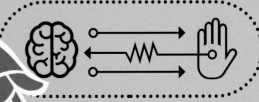

ANDROIDS

ANDROIDS ARE ROBOTS THAT ARE DESIGNED TO LOOK AND ACT EXACTLY LIKE HUMANS. FOR MANY YEARS, REALISTIC ANDROIDS ONLY EXISTED IN SCIENCE FICTION, BUT MODERN SCIENTISTS ARE GETTING EVER CLOSER TO DESIGNING LIFELIKE ROBOTIC HUMANS.

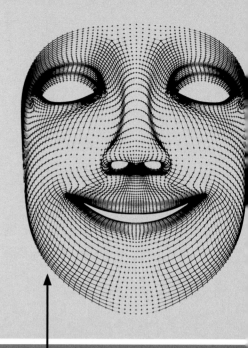

Robot designers use engineering and programming to make androids appear to have emotions, just like humans. Tiny artificial muscles, controlled by motors, are placed on the android's face. The muscles are programmed to move to create different facial expressions when the robot senses that it is the appropriate moment, using visual or spoken clues.

An android may make a happy face when it picks up words such as 'happy' or 'good', or when its facial recognition software recognises that another person has a happy expression on their face.

SCIENCE TALK

Unlike cyborgs, which contain real biological parts such as muscles or nerves, androids are totally synthetic. To make androids look realistic, scientists cover them in synthetic materials, such as soft, flexible silicone jelly, that look very similar to real human skin.

The Geminoid android (left) is modelled after a real person (right). The robot designers copied everything from him, including subtle movements and gestures.

People often find it easier to relate to robots if they have human faces. They are happier to interact with them and find them less intimidating than typical machines. However, robot designers need to be careful because androids can look very creepy if they look nearly exactly the same as a human, but not quite!

PROJECT

- Find ten pictures of 3D computer-generated human faces on the Internet and put them in order from least human-like to most human-like.

- Do any of the faces seem creepy to you?

- Where do they appear on the scale?

- Show the images to some friends and compare their reactions to your own.

0 1 2 3 4 5 6 7 8 9 10

" ART TALK

Human faces are one of the hardest things to get right when drawing, painting or sculpting, and it's no easier for a robot designer! Using proportion will make your artwork look more realistic. For example, the width of a head is about the same as five eyes in a line.

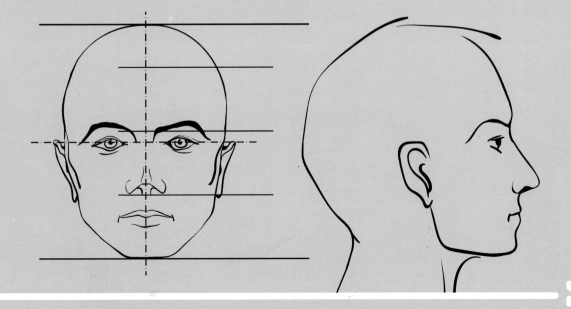

MANY OF OUR IDEAS ABOUT WHAT ROBOTS ARE LIKE COME FROM FICTIONAL ROBOTS FROM BOOKS, FILMS AND TV SHOWS. THE WORD 'ROBOT' EVEN COMES FROM A PLAY, WRITTEN BY THE CZECH PLAYWRIGHT KAREL ČAPEK IN 1920.

ROBBY THE ROBOT

This robot from the 1956 film *Forbidden Planet* was one of the first robots in film that had its own personality. Robby worked as a servant, but also enjoyed cooking dishes such as space doughnuts. For many years, Robby's shape inspired people's views of what a robot should look like.

C-3PO, R2-D2 AND BB8

These three droids (name for robots in the *Star Wars* universe) are designed to help their owners with various tasks. R2-D2 and BB-8 can repair and maintain spaceships, while C-3PO is an etiquette expert that can translate languages and explain foreign customs.

WALL-E

In the film of the same name, WALL-E is a rubbish compactor robot that is left to clear up a polluted Earth at some point in the future. Although WALL-E is programmed to carry out his duties, he also has a personality and hobbies, such as collecting things and owning a pet. These human characteristics make robots such as WALL-E appeal more to us.

TERMINATOR

This cyborg assassin from the *Terminator* films has no human emotions, but is practically impossible to tell apart from a human – he even sweats and bleeds! The story of the *Terminator* films is set in a future in which there is a war between robots and humans, with the Terminator fighting on the robot side.

DALEK AND K-9

These robots from the *Doctor Who* TV series appear at opposite ends of the good/evil spectrum! Daleks are evil, robotic cyborgs, made up of biological alien parts and artificial robot parts. The only emotion that they can feel is hate, which makes them a serious threat. Meanwhile, K9 is a friendly robot dog who makes an excellent companion to Doctor Who, just like a real pet dog.

OPTIMUS PRIME

This giant robot, seen in the *Transformers* films and range of toys, offers two looks for the price of one, as he can transform from a robot into a giant lorry! Optimus Prime is dedicated to fighting evil robots, to help robots and humans live peacefully together.

ROBOTS OF THE FUTURE

ROBOTICS HAS COME ON IN LEAPS AND BOUNDS IN THE LAST 50 YEARS, WITH ENGINEERS MAKING ROBOTS BETTER AT THE JOBS WE NEED THEM TO DO AND DEVELOPING THEM FOR JOBS WE WOULD LIKE THEM TO DO. IT SEEMS LIKELY THAT THE NEXT 50 YEARS WILL BRING SIMILAR PROGRESS.

The study of very, very tiny robots, or nanobots, is an area of robot research that could have an incredible impact on healthcare. Scientists believe that cell-sized robots could be programmed to go directly to areas with cancerous cells and destroy them, or be sent to repair damaged tissues inside the body. As the nanobots could be programmed to only target certain areas, they would help patients recover faster and more effectively.

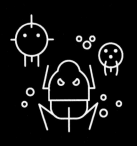

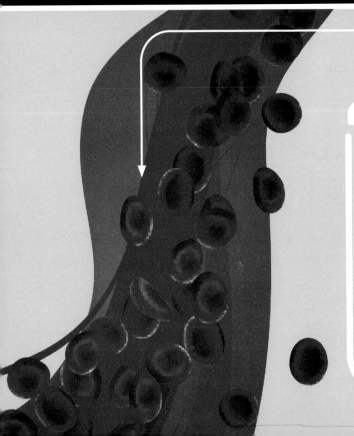

Scientists are looking into the possibility of a robotic red blood cell that could transport more oxygen around the body than biological red blood cells. This could help people with blood diseases or boost athletes' performance.

"MATHS TALK

Nanobots measure between 0.1 and 10 micrometres (for comparison, the width of a strand of spider web silk is around 3 micrometres). A micrometre is a division of a metre. There are 1000 micrometres in 1 millimetre, 10 millimetres in a centimetre and 100 centimetres in a metre. How many micrometres are there in a metre?

One of the greatest future challenges for scientists and robotics engineers is to perfect how to programme robots to behave in a typically human way. They have already created a robot nanny, Pepper, that is designed to babysit children and that can adjust its behaviour depending on the child's emotion. In the future, robots may be able to master jobs that require high levels of social interaction, such as teaching or working in the police force.

! ENGINEERING TALK

To recognise human emotions, the robot Pepper uses sound sensors and facial recognition software that identify voice tone and facial expressions. The robot refers to a database of common results to recognise the emotion shown and is programmed to react accordingly.

Pepper can respond to a human's emotions by displaying special symbols on its tablet and changing the tone of its voice.

THINKING OUTSIDE THE BOX!

Although many jobs that once belonged to humans may be lost to industrial robots in the future, the growth of robotics industry will also create more jobs. People with the right skills will be needed to design, test and build the robots of the future.

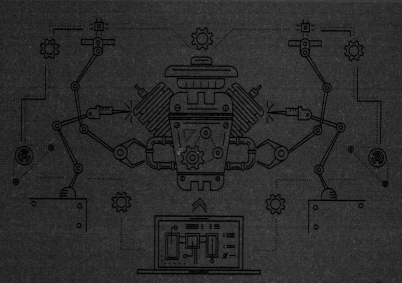

GLOSSARY

android a robot that looks like a human

artificial not natural, made by humans

artificial intelligence the area of science that deals with creating computers that can mimic human intelligence

automated not controlled by humans

biological something natural that is part of a living thing

cell the smallest part of a plant or an animal

circuit a complete circle around which electricity travels

code written instructions for a computer that explain how to carry out a task

cyborg a robot that has artificial and biological parts

database information stored in a computer in an organised way

ethics ideas about what is right and what is wrong

genetically engineered something that has had its genes changed by a scientist

GPS stands for Global Positioning System, a system of computers and satellites that work together to work out where someone or something is

humanoid something that looks like a human

industrial connected to the making of goods in factories

Industrial Revolution a period of time in the 18th and 19th centuries during which humans first used machines to do work, rather than doing it by hand

interact to communicate with and react to

molecule two or more atoms joined together (all substances are made of molecules)

navigate to find your way around

programme to give a computer a series of instructions

proprioception the sense of where your own body is positioned and how it moves

prototype the first model of a new product

radioactive containing energy from a nuclear reaction

sensor something that is used to sense (an eye is the sensor that we use to see)

sonar a system that uses sound waves for navigation

synthetic something that isn't made from natural materials

terrain land

tone the pitch and quality of a sound

FURTHER READING

A Robot World Clive Gifford (Franklin Watts, 2017)

How to Design the World's Best Robot Paul Mason (Wayland, 2017)

How to Build: Robots Louise Derrington (Franklin Watts, 2016)

WEBSITES

FIND OUT MORE ABOUT AMAZING ROBOTS AND HOW TO GET INTO ROBOTICS AT THE FOLLOWING WEBSITES

www.sciencekids.co.nz/robots.html

www.robotics.arc.nasa.gov

www.nationalroboticsweek.org/Resources

QUIZ

- Why do robots in space often run on solar power?

- Who wrote the Three Laws of Robotics?

- Name two ways in which the military uses drones.

- What animal does Paro look like?

- Which fictional robot has a job collecting rubbish?

INDEX

QUIZ ANSWERS

- They can't connect to mains electricity or have their batteries replaced.
- Isaac Asimov
- Some uses include surveillance, carrying weapons and dropping bombs.
- A seal
- WALL-E

BUILDINGS

- Starting out ■ Materials
- Structure ■ Arches and domes
- Designing a building ■ Scale and plans ■ Perspective ■ Ancient buildings ■ Greeks and Romans
- Castles and cathedrals ■ Architects
- Houses ■ Eco-friendly buildings
- Skyscrapers ■ Landmarks
- Public buildings ■ Bridges
- Famous bridges ■ Tunnels
- When things go wrong
- Hostile conditions

COMPUTERS

- A Computer is... ■ Computers everywhere ■ Ones and zeros
- A computer's brain ■ Memory
- Inputs ■ Outputs ■ Programming
- Early days ■ Computer scientists
- Software ■ Graphics ■ Games
- Personal computers ■ Networks
- The web ■ Virtual reality
- Artificial intelligence ■ Amazing computers ■ A changed planet
- Future computers

MATERIALS

- Choosing Materials ■ Natural or Manmade ■ Solid ■ Liquid ■ Gas
- Rocks and Minerals ■ Wood
- Metal ■ Glass ■ Building
- Plastics ■ Ceramics ■ Textiles
- Art ■ Composites ■ Chemicals
- Super Materials ■ Special Surfaces
- Shape Changers ■ Recycling
- Future Materials

ROBOTS

- Designing a robot ■ Moving parts
- Circuits ■ Sensors ■ Sight and navigation ■ Code ■ Programming robots ■ Artificial intelligence
- Robot ethics ■ The first robots
- Robots in danger ■ Robots in space
- Drones and cars ■ Real robots
- Household robots ■ Robots and medicine ■ Bionics ■ Robotic arms
- Androids ■ Fictional robots

SPACE

- Learning about space ■ Our solar system ■ Stars ■ Galaxies and the universe ■ Comets and meteors
- Black holes ■ The Big Bang
- Astronomers ■ Observatories and telescopes ■ Space exploration
- The science of space ■ Astronauts
- Training for space
- The International Space Station
- Space walks ■ Rockets ■ Rovers
- Space probes ■ Satellites
- Space colonies ■ Future exploration

VEHICLES

- Designing a vehicle ■ Land vehicles ■ Bicycles ■ Cars
- Famous cars ■ Trains ■ Watercraft
- Boats and ships ■ Hovercraft
- Aircraft ■ Aeroplanes
- Helicopters ■ Extreme terrain vehicles ■ Power ■ Materials
- Speed ■ Braking ■ Safety features
- Style ■ Record breakers
- Vehicles of the future